ANNUNAKI THE FALLEN ONES

Annunaki
The Fallen Ones.

"They who come from the stars."

Annunaki
The Fallen Ones.

Every story has a voice. It falls upon our shoulders to bear witness to the story and to act as contributors to developing its book thus to be its hands to fill its destiny. It's up to you, the readers what you want to take from a story, but I bet you won't leave behind any of the good stuff. Every story deserves to be heard thus to have an open ear and mind to come along with it. These things have complicated lives just like we do. The struggle to be heard is a tough battle for both of us but I'm sure if we work together we could be able to be heard.

Annunaki
The Fallen Ones.

Annunaki

The Fallen Ones

Back Again? 17

Who are they? 19

Where Did They Come From? 25

Which Religion is Right? 45

Star Seed 49

Annunaki
The Fallen Ones.

Every story and Myth started somewhere, but where exactly is the question. Some of them are mixed with a few truths.

Annunaki
The Fallen Ones.

"Arrogance sometimes leads to a lot of misunderstandings."

-Terrell L. Frazier

Annunaki
The Fallen Ones.

In theory, I believe that the Annunaki bloodline extends all the way back to the ancient king and queens of the ancient world, especially of those within the Ancient Egyptian and Sumerian royal families. There might be even the possibility that these bloodlines exist in their descendants that are spread all across the globe.

Annunaki
The Fallen Ones.

I'm no Zachariah Sitchen nor an Alien Enthusiasts, I'm just someone who has innate knowledge and experience in the subject. The Annunaki are known to me because they were and still are apart of me.

Annunaki
The Fallen Ones.

Acknowledgment

Zachariah Sitchen, Ancient Aliens

Honestly, I never read any of Sitchen's work because I didn't need to read them because I already knew about the Annunaki, but I will give credit where credit is due, and I'll give it to Sitchen. Also, I would like to give props to the TV show, *Ancient Aliens*, and all

Annunaki
The Fallen Ones.

the other shows. Thank you for proving something to be real that I once thought wasn't. Thanks to you I don't stand alone in this belief and there are many others like me who believe in these things. It's true what they say that you're never truly alone in anything now I see this now.

It appears that the Annunaki's backstory was a play in my early young life. But the saga that they played a role in was not an epic tale from the past but of the future, a future that we are bound to live or relive. This whole dream ordeal made me wonder if any of this coincided with my theory of Alternative timelines.

The Theory goes that possibility that there is more than one alternative version of the original universe

Annunaki
The Fallen Ones.

and we are amongst the many copies of the original. In this case, I think that we could be reliving a future that has already past and bound to relive.

I've talked about this on numerous occasions in my previous works. So, if you would like to get an idea of where I'm coming from then I suggest you read *2016 Again?* It's not the best piece of work but I tried to make a decent story to convey a powerful message I still hope that many would take heed to.

Even the bits of information about the Illuminati were available to me and I didn't realize it to me. The whole diamond hand gesture, I used to do to then in the shape of a tree thus sending signals to the sky hoping that the aliens could get my signal, which they did. My old

Annunaki
The Fallen Ones.

backyard was a strange place a lot of weird activity went on there. It's my belief that it was some sort of spiritual nexus, a crossing between multiple worlds and indeed it was. In my dreams, I used to believe that the symbol of black and white checkerboards was evil and that they were used by the elite forces to identify their slaves.

In this dream, the Annunaki had the people wore black and white clothing to allow everyone else that wasn't of their control that these people belonged to them. The people wore the same designs and same shoes it was almost like no one had no kind of color of their own. Meaning that they didn't have a style of their own to stand out from the rest they were, all the same, This was a rather tasteless outfit to me and sad. Luckily, I was one of the ones who stood out and wasn't a slave to the

Annunaki
The Fallen Ones.

Annunaki. Even in my dreams, I was so blessed. As time went on and more and more of my dreams become reality, it made me question myself. "Just what the fuck am I? I would think to myself. No, I'm not a prophet but I am an old soul. It's without a doubt that perhaps in one of my pasts lives that just maybe that I was one of them, that I was formally Annunaki. Hell, who knows, the way my family is so mixed up, I'm probably having this in my DNA, probably more than most people in the world. It still surprises me how much I knew before ever reading a book about the subject.

Personally, I like my theory of us being on an Alternative Timeline than ever being connected to the Annunaki. It just not one of those things that I would be proud to speak of. Whatever the case may be, I got this

Annunaki
The Fallen Ones.

knowledge from somewhere and even I don't know where I got all this information from. It would truly be an interesting thing to find out how and where but I'm guessing the only person who could give me a definite answer is my Higher Power.

Yes, I do have a mental illness, I was born with one. Since I was a child I was diagnosed with A.D.D which is also known as Attention Deficient Disorder. ADD is basically having an issue with staying focus in which I did a lot. This is an issue that I've struggled with for years but it's not the reason why I came up with this passage. Just because I'm mental doesn't mean that I'm totally crazy. My mental illness is one of my character defects and this is something that I had to learn to except.

Annunaki
The Fallen Ones.

It was hard growing up being teased because I was a little feminine, poor, and a mentally challenged child. All this was too much to bear and the people I was around were ruthless, yet I survived all that hell I went through. Today, I'm the epitome of everyone's hate being openly gay, African-American, an HIV-victim, and a mental case one would say that I am a walking mess. In many ways, yes, I'm a mess, but I'm also a beautiful soul and to me, that's what matters the most not all that extra stuff.

There are similarities between my maternal family and his own which makes me think that we are one big family. Perhaps this is so but this would be difficult to unearth. It doesn't matter to me but what

Annunaki
The Fallen Ones.

really matters is that I know now where it all started and where it began. After the fall of the 18th dynasty during the early Ramesside's era, one of the Amarna Princesses migrated from land to land thus ultimately began a new breed of Thutmosides which you see with me today.

"To understand me you must understand Tutankhamun, King Tut.'

Being able to study the true authentic part of my ancient family history, I've learned that my mental illness is hereditary and it's not only from my mother but from generations back, it's not my fault that I'm this way. Mental illness had long been encrypted in my

Annunaki
The Fallen Ones.

families since before the times of the 18th dynasty of Egypt and this is all because of incest. Believe it or not, we all carry a part of our ancestors whether it be millions of years or go on a thousand, a part of them still lies within. Incest has a long-lasting effect in this family and a result of this is mental illness throughout the generations of the bloodline.

    Not poking fun at anyone, but many of us suffer some mental and emotional issues that have resulted in us acting a bit unusual at sometimes, but we manage to keep afloat. My family is rather unique I can tell you that, they are extremely than most families. They may not get along all the time, but these people love to party. They have a celebration for just about anything, well some of us. Mentally challenged or not we still have a

Annunaki
The Fallen Ones.

love for one another even though we don't necessarily show it sometimes.

When you are dealing with someone who is Mentally Disabled, do no automatically wright them off as sick or silly because most of the time it's not their fault why they are the way they are. Try to understand them but please do not hurt them because their feelings are extremely brittle, trust me, because my feelings are the slightest thing that could hurt my feelings. I'm if this was the constant bullying that I was getting when I was a child. Bullying too could be a result of mental illness. One could be driven into depression or slightly insane with constant bullying. For me, I came from a very broken home and had to deal with outside forces from

Annunaki
The Fallen Ones.

the whole it was a lot to deal with as a kid and to be honest, it did a lot to me mentally. No child should come home to domestic violence, arguing, and down-right negativity then turnaround and be physically and mentally abused by peers, it was stressful. No one should have to go through what I did.

"Listen to understand not to Judge."

Try to comfort someone with mental illness and again, don't write them off because they are people and sometimes they are telling a lot of truths. Sometimes if you listen to them, I mean really listen to them you will get a good lesson out of them. We can be some of the

Annunaki
The Fallen Ones.

most life-changing people in the world and you could learn a lot of us just by simply listening.

This story is not something that was make-believe, though the subject, at one time I thought were. Now I know that they are very much real and are somewhere out there probably watching everything go down on Earth. In previous years, I used to believe in what others thought of myself, that I was completely insane but now I know that this is not even so. There are just simply beyond our comprehension.

"God grant me Serenity

to accept the things that I cannot change

Annunaki
The Fallen Ones.

the courage to change the things that I can
and the wisdom to know the difference."
Living one day at a time
Enjoying one moment at a time
Accepting hardships as the pathway to peace
Taking, as he did,
the sinful world as it is
not as I would have it
trusting that he will make all thing right
if I surrender to your will
that I may be reasonably happy in this life
and supremely happy with him
forever in the next, amen"

Reinold Niebur
(1892-1971)

Annunaki
The Fallen Ones.

Once again, I've found myself completely mystified by the star yet again. Every night as I look up to them, I wonder, wherein the deep dark skies do I belong. Now I know this may sound a little strange for me to say but I don't belong here. Apart from I always felt that I just didn't belong. Why was I even here in the begin with? I would ask myself and then I realize that the answer to the question had been given to me a thousand times and I wasn't even paying any attention to the answer.

Do you think that you are here just for yourself? My life wasn't mines alone it was for someone else. Jesus Christ was born to fight for the equality of all people and to die for our sins as the Christians would say and thus just like Jeshua, I had to bare scars so that someone else could be able to

Annunaki
The Fallen Ones.

understand my trials and tribulations so that they wouldn't fall, victim, as I have. Oh, what painful scars they are.

Even as this book was written, I was feeling seriously bad about myself. There has been so much stuff that happened to me over the years that I just don't know how I survived. As I wrote this book, I was sad, alone, hurt, broken-hearted and down-right defeated. My entire world was crumbling before me and I didn't know why, why am I going through this madness? Why was I ever born? When I was younger, I used to think that this reality could've been all just a bad dream that I could never wake up from. Over time, I wished that I could, but it seems like I'm so stuck and lost.

"WHY HAVE YOU DESERTED ME! I would cry out to go.

Annunaki
The Fallen Ones.

"*WHY DOES THE WORLD HATE ME!* I would've raged heavily.

It seemed like I was hated by everyone in the world as I was growing up. Everything that I lived through seemed to be the very thing that someone had spoken over me in the past. In a sense, I was living someone else's perception of me. Yeah, I fell hard as a victim to mental strife and abuse but now I'm climbing up to be amongst the highest of high. There will be more days that I will feel down and defeated, but I will have more control over this vessel that I'm temporarily using. It is for the love of this world, space, friends, and my beloved family. There is something special in me in all of us that Gods sees and had specially made for each one of us.

Annunaki
The Fallen Ones.

In a strange yet delighted way, I feel like I know where I belong now, it's up there in space in the stars where the angels and heavens are. No longer shall I believe that doesn't come from anything because there is proof in the stars that I'm specially made from various parts of the universe. Home is where the heart is and its space and maybe that is the energy that is drawing me to the majestic wonder above us.

My mission is to spread a story that I believe came from the heavens about a group of people of unknown people who are not native to this world at all. It's my belief that the divine order sent me these messages from the past and from the future to have me tell the tale of mankind's repetitive history. Thus, how if we're not careful, we could slip up and repeat the same fate as we did in the past. These

Annunaki
The Fallen Ones.

beings in which I've written about may truly be out there just waiting to seal our fates.

"The Universe is a living breathing thing as well. It was born, it eats, it procreates, and it goes through many radical changes with its body just like all organisms in the universe. It's a mass composed of life, yet its life remains a mystery. It has a soul, a heart, and a backbone just like we do to keep us all together. The Universe is a lifeform filled many smaller lifeforms and when we see it as such then we could better understand.

Annunaki
The Fallen Ones.

Back Again?

Way back in 1997, I used to have these dreams where mankind was all enslaved by this unknown force. Thus, I and a selected few were chosen to stop this unknown force and free the planet from slavery. We were a rag-tag group who didn't even want the slaves to touch us, in fear of infection or something but we had to place our differences aside from each other and save the planet.

The next morning, when I got to school, I just had to tell the other students. Back then I was attending

Annunaki
The Fallen Ones.

Fishburne Elementary School in Hanahan, South Carolina. This was a nice school but the children, oh my. Imagine being the only broke kid in the room full of children whose parents were rich, lawyers and you know, the whole elite shit. Meanwhile, your mom was living off government assistance and your father was never around, not a pretty life to display. It killed me to even try to fit in because it would've only made matters worse and made the kids hate me even more. Feeling like I was a part of the crowd and that the dream was somewhat important to us, I shared my dream with some of the kids.

"I had a dream that we all were slaves," I said.

'You're Weird." The little mixed kid looked at me as if I was some horrifying creature or something.

Ugh, I hated that little brat he always harassed my damn nerves. After this, I never talked about my dreams

Annunaki
The Fallen Ones.

to anyone, not even my mother because I would've been ridiculed for them. Unexpectedly, I transferred to another school and never saw them again but that wasn't the end of the torturing, but that's a story of another time. Overtime I would dream about these battles against these unknown forces in various carnations.

To be honest the dreams seemed more exciting than my actual life. Things changed drastically as I got older and sexual tensions grew I was no longer thinking about those things but a hard-plump cock. It was like those things were as they were figments of my imagination. However, I discover that this would not be so and the beings that I

Yes, I'm back and I'm again talking about the Annunaki. For those of you who did not know this, but I've talked about them in my last book and my reasons for me talking about them is because of my inner

Annunaki
The Fallen Ones.

knowledge of them. Like I've stated in my book *"2016 Again?"* the knowledge of the Annunaki was innate, I was born with this knowledge about these beings. As a child, I thought that they were all just figments of my very vivid imagination but later in life, around the age of twenty-two I've found out that there is a possibility that the Annunaki weren't a figment of my imagination and they were very much so real. Now, I'm going to tell you that this sent alarm bells off in my head because the knowledge that I had about them wasn't pleasant at all. As a matter of fact, they were crude and sickening.

Remember that Movie, "*the Fourth Kind.*" Well, even though the movie was fictional I believe that the aliens of that movie are the same ones that I am talking about.

Honestly, I swore that this movie was real it had me believe that it was based on actual events. Whoever

Annunaki
The Fallen Ones.

wrote that script was spot on about the Annunaki. They could really do those things that they did within the movie in reality. How do I know that those aliens were the Annunaki? Well do the research and when you find the similarities then you will get it.

Chapter One:
Who are they?

Annunaki
The Fallen Ones.

Depiction of the Annunaki.

Around 2012, When I was living with my grandmother, I've discovered s show called *Ancient Aliens*. As I watched the segment about the Annunaki, I said to myself, hmm this sounds very familiar and then that's when I realize that these are the people that I used to dream about when I was younger. These were the

Annunaki
The Fallen Ones.

alien invaders that had enslaved and will enslave the earth in my dreams, I thought to myself.

This discovery was very shocking and made me question myself. How did I know this stuff? Where did this knowledge come from? So many answers that I had yet I had to find the answers. Now, I think that the answers lie within myself, but I must dig a bit deeper than I was before. Despite my excitement about being right Annunaki, I was a bit concerned about the future I wondered if they returning? This is a story that I've already written. Anyways, I used to have strange dreams about Alien Invasions and the Annunaki often, but I could never understand them.

Being curious as to why I was getting these dreams, I decided to ask around to people whom I considered the wisest and was possibly able to provide an answer. Being the person that I am, I'm always open

Annunaki
The Fallen Ones.

to having my ear open to listen to other's perspectives and intake on certain things that I present to them. The first person was my then boss. Back then, I was working as a work-study at my local community college and although I wasn't the best worker, I really enjoyed working with the people at Virginia College especially my boss she always gave me insight about life and how true kindness works. This woman really got me together.

So, I told her about the dream that I had, and she told me to ask God about what he was revealing to me and what was in store for the future. What I found interesting was the fact that she called my dream a premonition of some sort. I was hoping to get a different answer because I didn't want this to be the outcome for humanity, but she assured me that everything happens for a reason and sometimes these things that happen are out of our control. She wasn't the last person who told

Annunaki
The Fallen Ones.

me this. Deep down and side, I knew that what she was telling was going to be an answer in some shape or form, but I wasn't satisfied I just had to have been wrong. Another friend of mine told me the Annunaki were my ancestors and that I cannot refute who they are to me. This was a tough pill to swallow because to me, the Annunaki were evil and I don't do evil. My friend was an older Caucasian woman whom I would speak to in passing whenever I walked by her house. This woman was funny as hell and always had a story to tell whenever she saw me, and I was always eager to listen.

    What I found interesting about talking to these ladies is that what they were saying perfectly aligned in what was said about the Annunaki in many theories and philosophies. They all left the conversations with the same message that I've always equated to the incident. That message was *"if we don't learn from our past then*

Annunaki
The Fallen Ones.

we are doomed to repeat it." This is one of those messages that would stand the test of time and would stick to all parts of our lives. Furthermore, it's a message that we must take heed to if we are to grow spiritually stronger. Their opinions allow me to understand a lot and discover how gifted that I'm truly am.

"In those days there were giants; and after that, when sons of God came unto the daughters of men, and they bare children to them, the same became mighty men which were of old, men of renown."

Genesis 6:4

The reason why this book is called *The Fallen Ones* is that I got inspired by the Nephilim, whom I believe to be The Annunaki. The Nephilim are said to be

Annunaki
The Fallen Ones.

the *"Heroes of old"* and the offspring of "the *Sons of God.* And the daughters of men. Some have equated the Sons of God as the fallen Angels those who were thrown out of heaven by God during the battle against Lucifer, a battle in which I called the battle of Beginnings.

According to the book of Enoch, the Nephilim were a race of giants and super-beings who committed acts of evil. This to me would align with my theory as well as the theories of others about the Annunaki. Let me rein form everyone who the Annunaki is and why they are so important to just about everyone on important to everyone on the face of the Earth.

The Annunaki were the gods attested in the Ancient Myths of the Babylonians and the Mesopotamians which dates back about 3600 BCE. The Annunaki are said to have descended from the heavens. In the ancient Sumerian texts, there are stories explaining

Annunaki
The Fallen Ones.

the Annunaki's activities, wars, and how they used to mate with the Earth People in those times. It's widely believed that the Annunaki are responsible for shaping Homo Sapiens Sapiens into what they are today. These Homo Sapiens being modern-day mankind. This has been written off as a complete myth and the notion of this is based on Pseudo-Archeology. However, there is no proof, either way, to prove that they did or didn't exist. Despite, how I feel about the Annunaki, they are responsible for genetically altering our DNA with theirs. So, in a way, many of us have Annunaki DNA. Me, I tend to think that I'm from another race apart from the Annunaki just to not have any association with them. The name Annunaki means that "They who came from the Heavens."

There are four major players in the Annunaki. Their names are An, Enki, Enlil, and Marduk. An, or

Annunaki
The Fallen Ones.

Anu, is the highest order of the Annunaki and is from an older Pantheon of the group he is first mentioned in the Babylonian texts. It states that an is a major authority figure, the decision-maker, and progenitor in which everyone hails from. An is credited to be the creator of the known universe in Babylonian beliefs. He's basically the Zeus of the ancient Semitic text and later came to share his power with his offspring.

Marduk is another popular deity from the text who rose from Obscurity in the Third Millennium. Marduk is said to be the patron God of the ancient city of Babylon. Marduk's symbol is the Mushussu or snake dragon. I've written about Marduk in my previous work 2016 Again? In this book one of his descendants had become a super-elite thus was one of the beings who led the people of Earth back into the hands of Enslavement.

Annunaki
The Fallen Ones.

Little is known about this God and what his function was in the pantheon.

Now, let's talk about the two most popular siblings in the text, Enki and Enlil. Enki and Enlil are brothers and the sons of Anu. These two are the best known of the Annunaki, even more so than their own father. Enki is said to be the mischievous god of wisdom, magic, and incantations. Lord Enki is also stated to be the one who resides in the ocean underneath the earth. There has been said that there is a second ocean within the Earth's mantle. How the ancient ones knew this information is very baffling to me. In the text, this ocean is called Abzu and it also was a very important place in the ancient Mesopotamian cosmic geography. In various accounts within the ancient text, Enlil is often depicted in sexual portrayals of his manly masculinity. Like, I've told you in the past, the Annunaki were overly sexual

Annunaki
The Fallen Ones.

and didn't mind having sex with their subordinates. Enki is also believing to have been the creator and the protector of mankind on Earth. Enki is also stated to be one of the most powerful deities in the Mesopotamian and Sumerian text

Enki's brother Enlil is written to be the one to decree the fates and his decisions could not be altered. In other words, it would've been extremely hard to change his mind. Enlil is also stated to be the god of air, earth, and water. Enlil is also the guardian of the *"Tablet of Destinies."* Which is supposed to be an ancient artifact that is said to be written in cuneiform, which is a written language created by the ancient Mesopotamians. Which are God who holds these would be the Supreme Ruler of the universe? These two infamous brothers are constantly spoken about when it comes to talking about the Annunaki and the creation of man. There was a tale

Annunaki
The Fallen Ones.

that these two are half-brothers were constantly fighting amongst each other overrule of the lands and that mankind have blood types each brother.

Personally, I don't think that I have any association with them and that I come from another race that is not Annunaki. Knowing that I know about them makes not want to claim that part of my history even it is true. Enlil is said to be the evil brother but to me, they all are very malevolent forces

Chapter Two
Where do they come from?

Annunaki
The Fallen Ones.

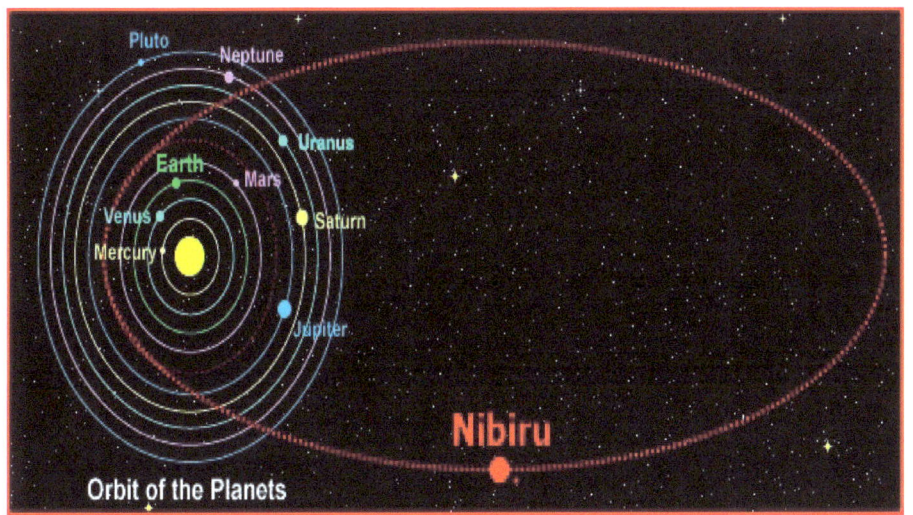

(I don't own this image)

The Annunaki are said to have come to a planet named Nibiru. Nibiru is Akkadian for moving or transitioning, and what a journey has it been on for the last thousands of years. Planet Nibiru is said to exist amongst the Oort Cloud in the outer Solar System. For many years there have been speculations of hypothetical

Annunaki
The Fallen Ones.

planets within that area of our Solar System and Nibiru is one of them. Recently, there has been news about a strange occurrence that was happening at the near end of our solar systems. According to notice that some objects within the Kuiper Belt, which is basically like a second asteroid belt that exists beyond Pluto. Astronomers had noticed that objects in that area had been shaken up in an unusual orbit. This gave the Astronomers the assumption that this mysterious disturbance in the outer solar system was caused by a ninth planet.

    Honestly, Planet Pluto will forever and always be the ninth planet of our Solar System in my mind and nothing will get me to change that. Truth be told, this new planet nine has been brought up before but back then it was known as Planet X. For some Planet, Nibiru and Planet X are one and the same and are moving in a very awkward orbit around the sun. Could this

Annunaki
The Fallen Ones.

mysterious "ninth planet" and Nibiru be one and the same? This we cannot give any evidence.

Despite it all, I do not think that Nibiru originally from our Solar System. My reasons why are because the Annunaki is said to be thousands of years advanced than we are on Earth which to me rules out the possibility of this planet being created in our very own universe. Nearly, all the planets within our Solar system had been formed around the same time shortly after the Solar System was created. So, in other words, the Annunaki would've have been as primitive as we are today. But, this wouldn't be the case if they came from another Star System.

It's my belief that the Annunaki originates from the Orion Constellation from the Rigel Star System. Rigel is the brightest star on Orion's Belt. This is just a theory, but I think that the Annunaki were thrown out of

Annunaki
The Fallen Ones.

their star system via an astronomical event or perhaps even by an even greater civilization greater than themselves, such as the Onidagu, whom I've written about in my book "*Possible Future*." It's a possibility. Hell, I thought that the Annunaki were made up figments of my imagination so why can't beings like the Onidagu exist? If the Annunaki were truly thrown out of their star system than one could say that they have really fallen from grace in some shape or form and thrown out by some unknown force. I also believe that Neptune's largest moon, Triton, comes from another part of the galaxy or another galaxy entirely. My idea of the Annunaki stemming from the Orion's Belt comes from the Pyramids of Giza.

If you look precisely at the pyramids, the three Pyramids are aligned up perfectly with Orion's belt. I'm not saying that aliens built the Pyramids, oh no, those

Annunaki
The Fallen Ones.

massive and mysterious monuments were built by sheer hands and force. The Gods that the ancient Egyptians aka the Kemetics weren't going to lift a finger but then did lend a hand in their creation in their own way. The Pyramids were built during the fourth dynasty of Egypt, which is well-known due to the pyramids. These massive monuments were built with respect to the pharaoh Khufu and his son Menkaure and his Khafre. The largest which is Khufu's pyramid is also known as the Great Pyramid of Giza. It's suggested that these tombs could possibly be the tombs of the deceased kings and their families. However, known of their bodies have yet to have been discovered within the pyramids. Many mysterious still surround the great pyramids of Giza. Even to this day Archeologists are still trying to figure out their mysterious. New mysteries have sprung up with the discovery of new chambers located inside one of the

Annunaki
The Fallen Ones.

pyramids. This is just speculation, but I think the Pyramids of Giza were perfectly designed to be just what they are mysterious so that mankind wouldn't unearth its secrets. There are still many secrets left un-noticed within that entire valley. Even I have stated in my very first book *"Memoir of a Lost Royal"* that I've known of a chamber. Will mankind can find them all? Only time will tell. I'm sure that whatever is found will re-write mankind's history all over again.

It's also my belief that the Great Sphinx also located in the Giza Plateau in Egypt is not originally Egyptian. Furthermore, I believe that the Sphinx had been adopted by the Kemetics, but it doesn't belong to them at all. The Great Sphinx of Giza was once believed to have been built within the same period as the pyramids of Giza, but scientists now believe that the Sphinx is much older than previously thought. Perhaps this

Annunaki
The Fallen Ones.

mysterious monument belongs to a group of unknown indigenous people of that land. Furthermore, I think that whoever resided in the Giza Plateau was not a civilization but a colony of another world. Before it was Kemet, it was something else and yes, they came and dominate the world until they were driven out either by a catastrophe or by those who had enough of their tyranny, but these are just theories of mines. Facts that have yet to have been proven to be truths.

    The idea of the original Egyptians was driven out by a catastrophe that brings me to my next point, the Great Flood. It's my belief that there was massive flooding in the Giza Plateau not by biblical proportions but by a natural one. It's my belief that the Great Flood occurred due to the melting of the last remnants of the Last Age. The Sphinx itself has shown some signs of water erosion around its body which could be signs of

Annunaki
The Fallen Ones.

some flooding in that area or some heavy rainfall. Whatever the case may be the Sphinx suffered some erosion from a large amount of water. I think the most crucial part of mankind's history has been lost during the events of this Great Flood thus the times of Genesis are a unique one and important one. The Sphinx has been around since before the end of the Ice Age, it's a survivor of a time long forgotten.

    Yet, one must wonder if there were giants, what happened to all of them? Where have they all gone? Or are they truly gone at all? This makes it very easy for skeptics to assume that there were no giants. I, however, think that to an ancient man they were giants, but they were super-human beings from a completely different world. Reading the history of giants, I've considered that most giants descended from some primordial order as if they were the first to be created before mankind on

Annunaki
The Fallen Ones.

Earth. This is a similar fashion in the story of the Angels or Nephilim in the biblical stories. I've found this to be rather compelling. In my own opinion, I think it's safe to pinpoint the biblical story of Noah just around a year or two before the end of the last Ice Age.

This is the only other explanation as to where would a large body of water would come from other than a catastrophic Tsunami that could've occurred. However, if that was the case then the Sphinx and or the Pyramids would've been desecrated. Furthermore, we would have seen larger amounts of erosion on the Sphinx not just in the areas of its legs.

The Ice was melting all over and this already may have caused some great concerned for the civilians at that time who probably knew that if this huge glacier were to melt even further then their hold world was going to be destroyed in which it did. Fearing for his life

Annunaki
The Fallen Ones.

and his families, Noah probably built his infamous boat in preparation for this day. Thus, took all that he could save so that they wouldn't perish with the old world. No matter how people look at the story of Noah and the Arc, I believe that this is a valuable and most momentous time in human history.

There has been mention of many giants crossed the borders and have been known in many different names. One group of giants called Anakim shares almost and similar sounding name with the Annunaki. According to the Tanakh, the Hebrew Bible, The Anakim were giants that descended from Anak, which were the forefather of the Anakim. The Anakim are also said to be the descendants of the Nephilim as well. The Annunaki were originally about twelve feet tall towering over the average man on earth. This could've very well changed, and they were able to reduce their height to match up

Annunaki
The Fallen Ones.

with our own. Who knows, perhaps the Annunaki walks amongst us and we don't even know it.

There is a lot of history still missing from our textbooks. A clear majority of the Earth's history is still very much lost. In opinion, I think that some of our historical records are missing on purpose and things that we thought we knew to be the truth aren't the truth. An example of this would be the burning of the Library of Alexandria and the recent destruction of the ancient monuments in Iraq. Someone clearly wants something to remain unknown. Will we ever know the history of our origin? The answer to this question is up in the air but we are getting rather to finding out.

Annunaki
The Fallen Ones.

Temple of Kukulcan

There are many pyramids that are found all around the globe. The most notable ones are the great Pyramids of Giza and the Mayan Pyramids also known as the Mesmo-American or the great pyramid of Cholula. In ancient times this pyramid was known as Tlachihualteptl which also means, *"Made by hand Mountain."* In theory, I think that these ancient

Annunaki
The Fallen Ones.

monuments are also ancient docket ports, airports for the Gods who were said to come from the stars.

Sleeping giants?

There are legends that these gods sleep within or around these ancient monuments. There has even been a tomb of Osiris, the Egyptian god of the dead, being found on the west bank of the ancient city of Thebes in Egypt. The Tomb of Osiris was thought to be a myth but in recent years, this has been proven wrong. It is unknown what was found in the tomb, but something was there. A sarcophagus interestingly made for a giant was found in this tomb. This sarcophagus was made from granite which also the same material of the sarcophagus that was found in the pyramids of Giza. Like those coffins, nobody was found, so it is claimed. It's my belief that the public was alluded by false information,

Annunaki
The Fallen Ones.

Meaning, that Archeologists aren't going to tell us normal folks everything that they know. It's as simple as this, there are just things that we will never know because the powers-to-be, the elite, will not allow us to have access to these things. They are afraid of us because if we knew who we were, then we would question their authorities. The term elite often refers to the bankers, the government, the Illuminati, the Freemasons, and any other rich and powerful person that could gain access to this type of lost history. They know, they all know but they pretend as if they don't. Trust me when I say that everything has its order in things. The powers-to-be are too powerful and enjoy their power. More so, they are enjoying their false reality and they will not allow anyone to alter this. I, myself is probably biting off more than I can chew just about talking about this but if I were to die or be ridiculed about this then I'm right.

Annunaki
The Fallen Ones.

However, I will say this though. The Elites don't even know that there even more outstanding discoveries hidden within their backyards. There are many giants that are sleeping underneath the lands that we are walking on today. All casts had been aside during the melting of the ice during the previous Ice Age. Forgotten just like the time that has been replaced by false evidence. We, ourselves, are resting upon many mysteries and secrets yet we fear to even know it.

Annunaki
The Fallen Ones.

Ziggurat of Ur
(I don't own this image.)

Another ancient relic that I think also holds a lot of hidden secrets is the Ziggurat of Ur. For those of you who don't know what a Ziggurat is, a Ziggurat is a massive stone structure that has been built in Mesopotamia in the ancient city of Ur. This monument was created by King Ur-Nanmu who dedicated this

Annunaki
The Fallen Ones.

Ziggurat to the god of the Moon Sin/Nanna. In theory, this was the house of the Annunaki thus this was the city of Ur was their new capital. The Ziggurat of Ur is more important than we think, and the Iraqi forces know this which is probably why they take heed in making sure no one trespasses in this area. Today, I still wonder, why is this Ziggurat still of some importance to them, are they hiding something there?

After carefully reviewing some pictures of the Ziggurat of Ur, it looks like a stage of some sort set up for the Gods to land upon it upon arrival from wherever they come from. It's a unique structure yet I wonder what secrets are buried, beneath or within it. I'm sure that we may never know what it holds inside because of the restrictions that the Iraqi government has over this area. One could seriously get hurt coming near this thing,

Annunaki
The Fallen Ones.

that is how vast this thing is being protected. Seriously, who lives in there?

You want to know who I think knows what's inside of there? Yes, you guessed it, the Elites. Of course, if they have access to our pockets they would have access to the old-world knowledge as well, just look at the Vatican, they aren't sharing any of their tea with us. But they have come forth with their belief that extra-terrestrials being able to exist. I mean come on, you must be ignorant and stupid that we are truly alone in this universe. The power is in the people and if we all wanted to know what's going on behind the scenes I think would be able to find out what we needed to know. Power comes in multiple forms remember this.

This has been an interesting topic to talk about and I'm sorry that I didn't write a whole chapter book on the subject. Truth is, I felt like I had to explain what I

Annunaki
The Fallen Ones.

already know about the Annunaki and what I believe about them, not to piggyback on the theories of others such as Sitchen and Ancient Aliens. Remember most of the knowledge of the Annunaki was innately there, mostly who they were and their actions the rest was upon collecting more data upon confirming their existence.

    This topic was a very important topic to me because I feel like we haven't seen the last of the Annunaki. Somewhere down the line, we will be seeing them again if they aren't already here. Personally, I think that they are already here just well-hidden amongst the population or well protected by the ruling parties of the day. All around I've felt as major shift going on in the world from this moment forward and some driving force is pushing things around. Some claim it to be the Illuminati trying to create their New World Order, but who's over the Illuminati?

Annunaki
The Fallen Ones.

When this book is published or gets attention, I'm probably going to get totally ignored and probably mocked by many, but it's okay. Sometimes the best stories are told by fools and they don't always tell lies. I just want people to understand that there are forces beyond ourselves that we have yet to comprehend or probably never will. We must get over ourselves before we can try to understand someone else and that's the bottom line. Do I think the Annunaki will ever return? Hell yes, and there were numerous dreams that have shown me such just like the one in earlier on in the story. Dreams tell stories that we cannot tell ourselves in are awaken state.

On Sunday, February 02, 2018, I had this weird dream. In the dream, I was returning home from either being away for a while or simply going on a trip. When I came back home I found that a huge change was

Annunaki
The Fallen Ones.

occurring was going on nearby the area I was residing. As the bus traveled along its normal route, I saw many people, specifically men on a very large construction site. On the corners, there were bus shelters, so I assumed that these men were working on a project that would benefit the love income people in that area, but I could've been wrong.

As the bus passed, I saw more construction workers, a lot of them being Hispanic, Latino, Middle Eastern, Caucasian, and African Americans. Some of them had their construction tools and they were playing them. One Latino was standing on top of something and was pointing a Chainsaw at one of his employees. From the looks of the workers, they weren't all that bright and were downright wild and beastly in nature. This could've very well been a symbolism of what mankind has become.

Annunaki
The Fallen Ones.

Eager to see this guy that I was madly in love with, I was searching wondering if he was on this site too. Frantically, I looked around hoping to spot him, but he wasn't. Finally, at some point, I got off the bus and looked around. Curiously, I walked around the construction site wanting to know what was going on and what was going to be of the area that they were working on. Along the way, I discovered another worksite, but it was near the edge of a large wide cliff which looked like it was high above the ground. As I walked toward it I got this feeling as if I knew what was down there at the bottom of the cliff and whatever it was it was extremely horrifying, and I didn't want to see what was down there or in other words, face the truth thus I ran for my life completely horrified about what I already knew was down there at the bottom of the cliff.

Annunaki
The Fallen Ones.

This dream started out fine until it got to the last part I could've felt the fear coming from myself as I approached the site near the cliff. This is one of the several dreams that I have been a lot of construction was going on and the people were forced to do the work. This gave the idea that perhaps what was beyond that cliff was something in reference to the future or the Annunaki because I already knew what was down there and whatever it was it wasn't pleasant at all.

Back in 2015, I had yet another dream of Alien Invasion. Everyone was running for their lives trying to flee. I and a few others, and a rather notable actor who was trying to redeem himself were part of this group who were trying to stop these beings from taking over the world. I and the others led many of the survivors to safety out of reach of the invaders until we could vanquish them. In the end, we wind up defeating these

Annunaki
The Fallen Ones.

beings and a huge world-wide celebration was held for us and we became notable heroes across the globe. From my point of view, I had grown fond of the celebrity and I assumed that we hooked up.

    Nearly a year after this dream I had two dreams related to the subject. In the first dream, two of my siblings and I were running away from the Elite and the Annunaki. The Annunaki had already gotten most of the world but not us. They created a huge massive stone wall to keep people from escaping. Thus, just as the wall rose, my siblings and I leaped across the stone wall making out of the Annunaki's grip to our Freedom. Immediately we thought that all was well until we realized that we had forgotten two people, my mother and one of my other siblings so I decided to go back to save them, yet the dream ended there.

Annunaki
The Fallen Ones.

My second dream is what I believe was going to be the cause of the Annunaki returning, the arrogance of man. In this dream, I was enjoying some time with family and some old friends. I was at my nephew's school watching him perform on stage. This was pleasant for a moment. When we got home the passageway to my sister's house was flooded. I never understood what this meant but the water was blocking our entrance and we all had to skip over it to get to her house. My interpretation is that there may have been massive flooding or a storm that came over and we were just recuperating from the storm or whatever it was.

    As we approach the house, we noticed that everyone around the apartment complex was going bananas. Either they were arguing or doing something that he shouldn't be doing. Amongst this guy was someone that I was attracted to once before. Now this

Annunaki
The Fallen Ones.

guy I talked about was who I based the character Pheo on in my book *"2016 Again?"* in real life, this guy used to appear in places that I would be which made me wonder if he was either a time-traveler or an Annunaki spy, but that's a story all on its own. Anyhow, he came out of his apartment all shirtless and from the moment he started to look at me he began to rub his muscles as if he was infatuated with me. I, myself was kind of disappointed and at shock as to why the people in this area were acting out of control. This guy was about to fight some other guy on the opposite side of the apartment complex.

    Above them, there was this huge honeycomb looking structure. Its combs blinked simultaneously, some at a time. Instantly, I knew what this meant and what this regarded. This was all about a familiar force that has been watching Earth's activity for a long time now. I'm not completely sure if this was the Annunaki

Annunaki
The Fallen Ones.

that was towering around the world, but it very well may have been. The story that was told in this story that during mankind's arrogance and self-destructive behavior, a force would spring out and take over. Despite the numerous times that I had dreamt about this I still rejected its content as impossible. This could never happen to the planet of Earth, never. Which foolish thoughts that I still have to this very day.

    In the second part of this dream, I was walking around in the darkness of night. As I walked around, I noticed that there was no one around at all and everyone seemed to have vanished or been somewhere else. I knew what was going on, yet I was un-phased by it. The dream led me to believe that I was heavily guarded, meaning that I was completely untouchable by the beings who held everyone else on locked down. My family was elsewhere away from harm's way while I managed to

Annunaki
The Fallen Ones.

come back home just looking for someone who may not be under the influence of the unknown force. This was a rather sad dream because it seemed like I was alone and there was nothing that I could've ever done to stop these beings. Still, I hope, that this remains only a dream and not a distant reality for us all.

    For those of you who don't know me by now, I'm a believer that dreams are stories that we cannot convey in our real life and that some dreams, like my own, could possibly be premonitions. Over time, I've had several of these premonitions which happened years after I foresaw them. To me, it appears I shaped my reality in some shape or form that is why things that I dreamt about are currently happening. One thing that I do not want to happen is the return of the Annunaki.

    When do I think that the Annunaki is returning? My answer is whenever we are ready. In two of my

Annunaki
The Fallen Ones.

books that it could be possible that they may make an appearance no later than 2026 but this was all for fiction, yet nothing is impossible. Truly, they could come at any time or at any place but it's my belief that the Annunaki aren't ready just yet to make a good come back we have a couple of years or a hundred before we make physical contact with our alien forefathers. Again, nothing is impossible in these times nothing at all. But, I will say this though, we did leave a window of opportunity for them to walk into.

What I want people to get out of this book is to just know. To know that we aren't the only one out here in this big old universe and we will never be. There is stuff out there that is beyond our comprehension and these beings are one of them. Honestly, I want future generations to know what they will be up against or encounter when they do cross paths with the Annunaki

Annunaki
The Fallen Ones.

because they will. Perhaps I might not live to see it but someone else will and I would like for whoever is reading this to study well about the Annunaki.

Should we even be concerned? Yes, I think that this a very important subject for all of us. It's sad that many people will look at this apart of Pseudo-history because knowing is winning half of the battle and if you know what you're up against, you are most likely to succeed. I could only imagine mankind's future faces when they see these beings finally coming out of hiding and making physical contact with us. The world is going to go crazy and yes there will be the clear majority that would feel terribly threatened by these unearthly beings. The first encounter is not going to go well at all, I'm sure of it.

The media would be all over it and each people would be totally glued to their screens or running for

Annunaki
The Fallen Ones.

their lives away from these aliens. I mean who is ever ready for an unexpected guest? It's going to take some time for mankind to come to grips about Aliens. There will be those ignorant folks and people wondering how they could fatten their pockets elsewhere beyond Earth it's going to be a mess. I'm trying to stir away from the events of my previous works but it's not out of reach. I just hope the future man doesn't make any of that story into existence but then again, we are already doing this just in these times. Bigotry and discrimination will be at a whole new level, I'm telling you. There will be times of indifferences but there will be times of equality and peace. Perhaps I could be wrong about the following and everything would work out fine honestly, I'm hoping it would.

Just to be even more honest with myself, I know that I'm going to get seriously ridiculed for this belief.

Annunaki
The Fallen Ones.

Some would refute my claim and class me like an idiot and mental case thus to put my books in the back of the bookshelf. This going to be a tough burn and I'm not good with failure. However, to the few that will be listening, I thank you and I would like to tell you to never stop searching for answers until you get them. Mind you that some things are better left as secrets but if there is an open question, it's up to you to answer it.

They are here with us. Hiding amongst us in plain sight. They could be right there in front of us and we wouldn't even know it. They can turn invisible via their highly advanced technology and they could connect with anyone of us with Telepathy. The Annunaki are far beyond our comprehension but they aren't invincible.

"God, thank you for giving me the power of Knowing. It's a beautiful yet scary gift yet I embrace it as a gift

Annunaki
The Fallen Ones.

that you have given me since birth. Thank you for choosing me to hold this gift."

Ever since I was young I've always felt as though that Society was given the authentic truth and somethings were kept as secrets. Almost always I felt like we were pawns playing a vital role in a larger game. I felt like we all being controlled somehow, and we didn't know it. Everything that people are just getting aware of, I've always been aware of since I was a lad.

To me, to be consciously aware and awaken means to know and understand truly how all things work all around us. Not within a racial aspect but all prospective. I've been aware of a very long time now and it bothers me sometimes when people claim to be "woke." Because they only seek to understand one cause not many. Something has been going on since the 90s or

Annunaki
The Fallen Ones.

even earlier on and people are just now starting to awake to the truth.

This whole New World Order phenomenon is not a new subject, at least not to me. Although I didn't know what to call it at times, I knew that something dark was going on behind the scenes and we all just are paying roles in this big old play.

Due to constant bullying, I was a very paranoid person but not just in fear of someone hitting me but for other reasons. There was something off with the world's government and it made me grew not to trust it. As paranoid as I was, I used to think that the Government or the F.B.I was monitoring us from a satellite in space or some top-secret base somewhere. Being extremely cautious, I tried to keep the lights off, fearing that the government was tampering with our electronic devices to spy on us. Even with insects, I was very wary thinking

Annunaki
The Fallen Ones.

that they too were just artificial creations to spy on us. This may sound silly to you readers, but nothing ever surprises me anymore so it's a possibility.

When it came to certain foods, I would be cautious of what I eat and if the food looked a bit off, I wouldn't eat it or would throw it away. No one was going to alter my body or put something in it to make it die. Unfortunately for me, it was my own doing that has caused my health to be endangered. You can't trust anyone to treat your body as you treat it yourself.

Certain smells of the air often kept me alarmed. If I would smell something strange in the air, I would cover my nose with my hands and shirt fearing that something was in the air that was hazardous to our health. Now, with the constant use of Chemtrails, it seems like I was right. It appears that even breathing fresh air these days is dangerous to the body because we don't know what we

Annunaki
The Fallen Ones.

are even breathing in. Chemtrails are long-lasting condensation trails left by planes that are left behind planes that fly high in the skies. Some believe that these trails are fueled with bio-chemicals that has a strange effect on the biosphere and how people were acting from day today. Some say that this is just false allegations but even the legendary Pop Star Prince talked about Chemtrails in one of his interviews and to be honest, this is how I first learned about chemtrails is because of him. Prince seemed to be a person who understood was going on in the world and I'm glad that we had someone of his caliber to bring this subject to our awareness.

As I listened to his music and Michael Jacksons there were messages in their music which made me wonder what all they knew. There is still a lot of speculation around their deaths and to be quite honest, I'm one of those people who sort of believe the hype

Annunaki
The Fallen Ones.

surrounding their deaths. It's just so much stuff that we may never hear until years later of what really happened or perhaps we may never know what happened at all.

There is an idea that many celebrities are subjects to MK Ultra. MK Ultra is some mind-control program that was created in the 1950s. this program was used to interrogate and torture those who fell victim to it. Now, I do believe that MK Ultra is being used to an extent via music and anything within the entertainment world, but this is just my opinion. Like I've stated before, I feel like Celebrities are the most vulnerable to succumb to things like this and don't know it because they have an image to the public to uphold. Whereas we regular Joes and Jill's would be a bit harder to control.

Despite all these conspiracy theories, the bottom line is that there is something dark and twisted occurring in the world. Some would say that its all the doing of the

Annunaki
The Fallen Ones.

secret society of the Illuminati. This could very well be possible, but what or who is driving them to do so? There is something going on underneath our very eyes and we probably will know later in our lives as to what is happening.

    As much as many will debunk this, the Annunaki is a part of every culture in some shape and form. Even today, we sort of fashion after our forefathers and the Pleiadeans, who are these Nordic-looking beings that are said to come from the Pleiades constellation. Honestly, I think that the Annunaki truly came from the Orion constellation put were pushed out. So, in a sense, they have truly fallen from their graces. The biggest question is how were they pushed out and what pushed them out? This is an even bigger mystery all. I want to finish off this novel with this a quote written in a code made in a crop circle known as the Crabwood Circle it reads.

Annunaki
The Fallen Ones.

"Beware the bearers of false gifts and their broken promises. Much pain but still time. (Belief) it is good out there. We oppose deception conduit closing."
-Unknown extraterrestrial source.

Chapter Three:
"Which Religion is Right?"

Over the span of Human Creation, there have been many religions. All have similar beginnings and some serving the same purpose. Now, only three of these religions remain supreme and that is Christianity, Islam, and Buddhism. A vast percentage of the world's

Annunaki
The Fallen Ones.

population is either-or. But my question to these followers to the different fates, which religion is right?

Over time, I'm always this phrase from many Christians, *"God is the Way."* My questions are to you Christians is if this is so, then how you tell this phrase to other people who don't believe that your God is the way? I'm not trying to tell anyone to change their beliefs. I'm only asking for people to think, just sit back and think about the question. This might be right in someone's point of view, but I think I got an answer to my own question. To me, the answer is simply to be that what you are which is human. Human is all that we could be and born to be. It doesn't matter what you identify as you're still a human being.

Annunaki
The Fallen Ones.

"As long as there is Free-will no one could have absolute control over you."

The Annunaki may have spliced their DNA to alter the likeliness of the Human Population on Earth, but the creator of all things created even they. Whatever it is or whatever you want to identify as it exists in each one of us. Again, whatever that you want to identify it as this all-powerful entity exists, I know it because I experienced it for myself tenfold.

"I see as my Father sees."

What this quote means for me is that like my Creator or whomever we identify it as, I see the beauty of all things. The very essence of the small and large, the light and the dark. Sometimes I wish that I wasn't the only one with *God's Vision*. It's a very beautiful sight to even have. In theory, I believe that we are the Fallen. In

Annunaki
The Fallen Ones.

the story of the battle of Lucifer, God casts out his beloved angels which were a third of the stars within the heavens, a third. There is an infinite number of stars out there in the Multiverse.

Some might say that these beings were cast into Hell, a plane of punish me, fire, and brimstone but not all of them. Look around you. Yes, there is a possibility that many of us fell into parallel universes or plains and some of it may not have made it into the plane of the living, hence ghost and demons. These were entities that may try to come in via possession and other ways but never could truly grasp the world of the living. They are stuck between realities and can't get out. A third of the stars that to me equate to the number of living souls that could possibly be living in the Multiverses.

All we want to do is just live. Live our lives possibly as we did in the beginning, free of rules

Annunaki
The Fallen Ones.

restrictions and each other own expectations of how our lives should be. It's a reality that has long been forgotten but not impossible to reach. We've been to heaven before, but we seemed to have all forgotten that we started there.

Writing this story sure felt as if a huge weight has lifted off my shoulders. It's a weird feeling as if I was carrying a burden upon my shoulders for years and now that burden has been lifted off me. This is how I know that this story was supposed to have been told all along and not it's being told in book form. I'm not sure what would become of this information, but I hope that what is given can be taken from another perspective and everyone just sits back and thinks about the subjects at hand before they judge or ridicule.

Annunaki
The Fallen Ones.

"Some Fates just cannot be changed."

In my stages of writing my last few books, I was in a state of grief. Time to time I've found myself concerned about my niece and nephews and the world than my own self. It's daunting to know that we are destroying ourselves and there is little that I can do about it. In these times things seemed to have gotten worse and more and more violence has spread like wildfire. It's just out of my reach and out of my hands to change the world. I'm beginning that this is some sort of plan to allow that the Elites put to gain control over the population, but I could be wrong and that the World has taken a turn for the worst all own its own. All I must say that we must learn from our past mistakes or we are surely doomed to repeat the past. The ancients knew this

Annunaki
The Fallen Ones.

and time and time again, it has been shown this. We must do better or someone else might show us how.

However, I do believe that for each one of us to stand together, we all must suffer together. Okay, so we don't necessarily need an alien invasion to occur but whatever it takes to change the world to allow us to rethink what we are doing and to once again prove ourselves what it means to be kind human beings on Earth. We are truly lost, and I've found myself asking this question, *"What are we doing?"* really what? Things must change but as I said earlier in this passage, for us to come together we may have to suffer together.

The Annunaki are a topic that I believed that I once lived through either by a past life or some other incident. Knowledge of them has been imprinted within my brain and I cannot explain how that knowledge got there and why is it so important that I remember them.

Annunaki
The Fallen Ones.

Could it be that this was the case all in all? To remember them so that future man would know about them and just how important that they are to us all? Therefore, to warn of a past that seems to be doomed to repeat itself? This looks like the answer to my question, yet I hope I'm wrong about everything.

Chapter Four:
Star Seed
"Home away from Home."

Annunaki
The Fallen Ones.

**Depiction of a star child reaching out to the stars.
(I don't own this image)**

Annunaki
The Fallen Ones.

Before all this occurred in my life I wasn't sure if I was a bit crazy or just out of sync with the rest of the world. For many years, I've felt like I just don't belong in this world. Even as I
wrote this passage the feelings are imminent. This place is not where I belong, and I just seem out of place. Not necessarily feeling like I belong in this plane of existence. This could very well stem from my battered self-esteem at the times but even when I'm sort of at my highest, I feel this way. There is something about me that was very odd and out of touch with Earth and I didn't why it was like that, why was I not like the rest of my peers? Why was I not born normal like the others?

Am I truly an abomination that is walking amongst the Earth? What could it possibly about Terrell that is different from the others? These were some tough

Annunaki
The Fallen Ones.

answers that almost became facts by listening to other's opinions until I discovered the truth about what I really was, a Star Seed. A Star Seed is a person or persons who experienced life elsewhere in the universe other than Earth. There are many types of star seeds that can be identified.

The first is the Old Star Seed, which I identify as. The Old Star Seed is someone who has had about one-hundred lifetimes on the Planet Earth that could've expanded all the way back to the very beginning of Earth's history. Old Star seeds are referred to as the guardians of the Earth and have a strong link to Sirius, who is a spiritual guardian of Earth and Humanity. This previous sentence is one that I find the most interesting because if you remember in my latest books I talked about the Tituns of Titus. As a matter of fact, I talk about them or at least try to incorporate them into my work so

Annunaki
The Fallen Ones.

that I could create a group of self-less beings who could help put the planet back in order. To me, this was my divine person to protect the Earth and galaxy. When I used to be a kid I used to dream that this used to be what I was destined to do, watching power rangers and things like that. But it wasn't until a show called Digimon Adventure is when my drive to want to protect the earth and fight evil became fully charged.

One could say that that show Digimon Adventure was a show about Star Seeds who were pre-destined to save the world. I absolutely loved the message conveyed in the anime. Although it was a kid show it had some adult themes to it and it got older and new versions of the show came out new star seeds were introduced, and it seems like it was millions of the Digi-destined in which they were called in the anime, that was battling evil and protecting Earth. The same could be said about us Old

Annunaki
The Fallen Ones.

Star Seeds, minus the Digital Monsters. Now I truly understand where that idea originated from, from my higher purpose in life.

Old Star Seeds sometimes take the role as Spiritual Teachers, Shamans, Prophets, Light Workers, Temple Guardians, priests, and priestess, and would fill in all type of Leadership role. This something that I don't really designate with because I don't like to play a leader because it's too much of a responsibility. However, I will make a charge if it's necessary. I've reincarnated as the firstborn so I'm a natural-born leader and then I do tend to take the lead when I feel like things are taking a shift for the left.

Us Old Star Seeds are quoted to hold wisdom or knowledge of the ancients which was used on Earth. This part was also intriguing and finally, a light bulb went off in my head. Oh my God! This is where the knowledge of

Annunaki
The Fallen Ones.

the Annunaki came, from my past. Perhaps somewhere down the line, I was Annunaki or me was someone on the outside that dealt with them. I would like to lean towards the second part because If I was Annunaki, I wouldn't be writing against them and fearing them instead, I would be embracing them as if I'm part of the family. Thankfully, I'm not part of the clique.

Even though I don't know if this is true, I do believe that in a past life, or alternative life, I was someone who fought heavily against the Annunaki. Thus, possibly part of an Intergalactically organization that sought to remove the Annunaki from Earth. Perhaps, we succeeded and won the battle against the Annunaki. However, I don't think the battle was finished yet and it has yet to be over. Another idea is that maybe that in the future I've dealt with them and relayed information from my future self. For a better understanding of this please

Annunaki
The Fallen Ones.

my book *"2016 Again?"* you would totally understand where I am coming from. Discovering this makes me want to shout out Mystery Solved! About where this unknown knowledge came from in the first place. There are still many questions left unanswered and I'm dying to know more from the stars.

It is stated that this is the last life for many of us Old Star seeds who have completed their life cycles on Earth. Does this mean that we will be reborn elsewhere? I would hope so. I've found this bit to be very interesting as I do wish that this life be my last life on Earth. This place is getting way out of hand and has been too much to bear and I could be elsewhere where it's less dramatic and chaotic. I will continue to try to do my best here but that is all I could do. In secret, I've talked to God stating "Lord, please don't bring me back here again." Only bring me back here if I'm needed." I've asked of him.

Annunaki
The Fallen Ones.

Thus, I've said to myself that I will reincarnate but not on Earth however, I would like to be around in some shape and form to help assist it in its battle to be cleansed of evil, but these people need to learn a valuable lesson without the assistance of the Old Ones, the old souls, and to learn it on their own. I'm not sure if God heard me but I think he truly understands where I'm coming from with this. Yes, I do not want to come back here at all you can have that. But I will be around, oh trust and believe you will see me again. Who could forget this lovable smile and bucked-teeth?

Old Soul Seeds are also noted to have mastered the ability to be grounded and spiritually aligned. In this aspect, I try my hardest to do not losing my principles and I believe but holding them tight like a rod. Therefore, we Old Star seeds resonate with our extraterrestrial origins despite us being incarnated here on multiple

Annunaki
The Fallen Ones.

occasions. They say that home is where the heart is and my God, whoever said this is right.

The second group of Star Seeds is called the New Star Seeds or what I dubbed the "Freshly Planted Ones." Unlike us Old heads they had fewer lies on Earth than we did. These freshly planted seeds are attracted to the Earth and Humanity at the time of Ascension and it is now easier for each of them to integrate with humanity now than in their previous lives. In opinion, I think that these are the people are doing the negative altering with the Earth. Granted that they are young souls or younger in this plane of existence, they haven't learned as many lessons as we Old Star Seeds have which I believe is why we are having these major turns of events going on. The new Seeds are said to be young and often credited to be Crystal or Rainbow Children. Their lifetimes are the beginning of future cycles on Earth and they are

Annunaki
The Fallen Ones.

preparing for them. Good luck with this guy! Again, I think they are the ones that are turning the tables in recent times. I, myself, think that they need to learn as much as they can and we old Seeds cannot simply provide them lessons simply by words but by something else so that is why I think it's best for them to learn by experience and I'm probably not the only one who feels this way. We all have a purpose in life thus a purpose in being here what that is, is up for each and everyone one of us to figure on our own or with some spiritual help.

Here are some characteristics of a Star Seed. First starters they have a strong interest in spirituality. We also can spiritually grow when needed because have done this before. Secondly, we have this realization that Planet Earth is not our original home in which I always feel like. I'm kind of homesick in the way like I need to go home, and home is not here on Earth. Wherever it is, I

Annunaki
The Fallen Ones.

feel like that I cannot rest until I find it. Thirdly, we feel drawn to the outer-space, the stars, and science-fiction. Our qualities are being artistic, sensitive, and having possession of high consciousness. I am all the above. Star Seeds could live a difficult and challenging life. This is true because since birth I've lived a life of constant struggle and hardships and it appears that there wasn't any end of the suffering. Despite it all, I've learned a lot in my days of anguish and distress, there is hope for all of us. There is a beginning and there will be an end, therefore, all my suffering, worrying, and struggling will come to an end.

Star Seeds may often have dreams about places not native to Earth. Like me dreaming about Planet Sylvia as a child. A part of me, whole-heartedly, believe that it is out there lurking in the shadows of space or right before my very eyes and I don't even know it. We

Annunaki
The Fallen Ones.

also could experience both non-physical and Physical encounters with star guides and UFO. Which I have in the past. Finally, we Star Seeds have gifts off in the areas of healing, channeling and psychic sensitivities. It's hard to explain sometimes I could pick up a feeling from someone or read someone by looking in their eyes, it sometimes is intense moments, so I try not to consider the person's eyes sometimes. If you have any of these qualities, then it is possible that you could be a Star Seed. There are so many of us planted around the Earth, around the galaxy and to think we are all here to serve a purpose, to assist each other in spiritual growth. It's like I've stated earlier on in the book, I don't live for myself I live my life for someone else and this seems to be the absolute truth.

Finding this out allowed me to figure a lot about myself. Truly, I'm unique but one question still lingers.

Annunaki
The Fallen Ones.

If the Annunaki are my past, then why are they so important to me to know who they are and what they stood for? More so, what I would like to know is this information is something that is needed for the future and what is to come? The future has many faces or hats, yet it doesn't know which one that it wants to where yet. Let's hope that it decides to where one that has a better outcome for us all in the end.

    I'm so glad that I could write this story. Trust me when I say a huge burden has been lifted off my shoulders upon writing this. Honestly, I don't know what will become of me or this story after I'm gone but I hope that people could listen up to what I got to say because there may come a time where this information is needed. It may not be now in recent times or a few years down the line, but one day we will know the truth and that we cannot run from it at all. Just know that we come from a

Annunaki
The Fallen Ones.

greater place beyond our selves and beyond this plane and that we all are somehow linked to it. We will all get to it again, one sweet day but as of now, we got to focus on the mission which is the mission to live for each day thus to learn each lesson, to learn from each other, and to take care of this planet as much as we can. We could do this if we try to do so. There is a lesson in all this and we will one day learn of it in time so be prepared for it. Just remember that though times may seem hard and that there may seem like there is no end to the agony there is hope and if you keep the faith things will get better. Standing united than divided is the final lesson on Earth and I hope we all get to master this lesson once and for all. My name is Terrell Leonardo Frazier, thank you for allowing me to share my story.

Annunaki
The Fallen Ones.

"A Fool sometimes tells no lies."

- A common Fool (Me.)

www.ingramcontent.com/pod-product-compliance
Lightning Source LLC
Chambersburg PA
CBHW042340150426
43196CB00001B/6